THIS DESIRABLE PLOT

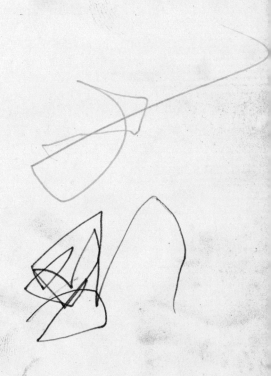

THIS DESIRABLE PLOT

A DREAM-HOUSE HUNTER'S NIGHTMARE

thelwell

EYRE METHUEN

First published in 1970 by Methuen & Co Ltd
11 New Fetter Lane, London EC4P 4EE
© 1970 by Norman Thelwell
Reprinted 1971
First published in this edition 1974 by Eyre Methuen Ltd
Printed in Great Britain by
Fletcher & Son Ltd, Norwich
ISBN 0 413 31880 X

Some of the situations depicted in this book are based
on my contributions to Punch *over the years and I am*
pleased to acknowledge this fact.

CONTENTS

" I WISH WE'D NEVER COME TO LIVE IN THE GREEN BELT. "

KNOW YOUR JARGON

IN MUCH SOUGHT-AFTER VILLAGE ...

IN A QUIET BACKWATER...

AMID COMPLETELY UNSPOILED COUNTRY...

A SUPERIOR FAMILY RESIDENCE...

OVERLOOKING THE PARK...

WITH PARTLY WALLED GARDEN...

... AND DELIGHTFUL SUN LOGGIA

A PROPERTY OF IMMENSE CHARACTER

WITH DIRECT FRONTAGE TO THE RIVER

CONVENIENT FOR
CHURCHES ...

VERY CLOSE TO SCHOOLS ...

HAVING SEMI-RURAL ASPECT...

NEAR TO FAST, MAIN LINE SERVICES

A PARADISE FOR GOLFERS

IDEAL FOR RETIREMENT

HANDY FOR COMMUTERS

WITH MAINS ELECTRICITY AVAILABLE

THIS PROPERTY AFFORDS FASCINATING POSSIBILITIES...

A KEY IS AVAILABLE FROM THE HOUSE OPPOSITE

MEET THE AGENTS

" YOU'LL BE AWAY FROM THE RAT RACE OUT HERE, MRS. LEGGIT. "

"THE PLACE NEEDS DECORATING, OF COURSE."

" THIS IS WILLIAM AND THAT'S MARY "

" LIKE I SAID, IT'S ALL READY TO WALK INTO."

"I THINK YOU'RE GOING TO BE LUCKY!
HERE'S SOMETHING THAT'S JUST COME IN."

"WOULD YOU MIND RINGING THE OFFICE
AND TELLING THEM I'M STUCK IN THE PRIEST-HOLE?"

" I WARNED YOU NOT TO LOOK DOWN, MRS. FRIMLEY. "

" ... AND THIS IS THE RECEPTION ROOM."

" ALLOW ME TO SHOW YOU THE SAUNA BATH, MISS HIPKISS."

" THE POOL HEATER'S A BIT ERRATIC "

" I'M SURE YOU'LL BE DYING TO EXPLORE THE GARDEN "

" I'VE SHOWN YOU EVERYTHING ON OUR BOOKS. ANYWAY,
WHAT'S WRONG WITH THE PLACE WE'RE LIVING IN NOW ? "

OWNER'S ANGLE

"THEY DON'T MAKE CEILINGS LIKE THAT ANY MORE."

" THAT'S NOT RISING DAMP. IT'S BEEN THAT HIGH FOR YEARS. "

" WE'RE WAITING FOR A BATHROOM GRANT FROM THE COUNCIL. "

" YOU'RE BOUND TO GET A BIT OF SHRINKAGE WITH CENTRAL HEATING.

" THAT WARDROBE, BY THE WAY, IS A FIXTURE "

" PLEASE DARLING!
LET ME SHOW THEM
THE MASTER BEDROOM."

" IT WOULD BREAK OUR HEARTS TO SELL FOR LESS,
OUR DOGGY'S BURIED HERE. "

" IT'S FIRST RATE LAND
FOR A WATER GARDEN "

" IT'S EITHER AN
ALTERNATIVE
WATER SUPPLY
OR A WASTE
DISPOSAL UNIT. "

" I DISTINCTLY SAID, VIEWING BY APPOINTMENT ONLY. "

" I WARNED YOU THAT THE STAIRS WERE A BIT STEEP. "

" WE'RE READY TO ENTERTAIN OFFERS OVER TWENTY THOUSAND. "

" MAKE ME AN OFFER "

BUYER'S TECHNIQUE

" GOOD AFTERNOON! YOUR NOTICE BOARD'S GOT WOODWORM. "

" HELLO! THESE JOISTS FEEL A BIT SHAKEY."

" DO YOU MIND IF WE POKE ABOUT ON OUR OWN ? "

" ALL RIGHT, I ADMIT IT! YOU CAN'T SWING A CAT "

" I SEE YOU'VE ALSO GOT YOUR OWN OIL-SLICK "

" IT DIDN'T HAVE DEATH WATCH BEETLE WHEN WE CAME IN . "

" WE'RE VERY TAKEN WITH YOUR ROOF GARDEN "

" SOME FRIENDS OF OURS HAD ONE OF THOSE AND IT BLEW UP. "

" SHE LEFT WITHOUT MAKING THE BED "

" IF THERE'S MOISTURE ABOUT, FRED WILL FIND IT. "

DO YOU COLLECT ANTIQUES?

" I DON'T THINK MUCH OF THE SUB-SOIL ."

" I TAKE IT WE'RE APPROACHING THE SEPTIC TANK ? "

" THAT DOOR'S GOT CHARACTER, OR HAS THE DOG BEEN AT IT ? "

STRUCTURAL SURVEY

" WATCH THAT POPLAR TREE START TO SWAY. "

" THAT BEAM IS FAIRLY SOUND, I'M HAPPY TO SAY. "

" I WARNED YOU NOT TO KEEP PULLING AT THE WALL PAPER."

" IT'S MENTIONED IN THE DOOMSDAY BOOK BUT VERY SCATHINGLY, I'M AFRAID."

" WE CAN'T FAULT THEM THERE !   IT'S A WELL STOCKED GARDEN ."

" LET ME PUT IT THIS WAY,
I WOULDN'T WANT TO
LIVE HERE WITH A WOODEN LEG."

" YOU'LL NEED A NEW COVER ON THE CESS-PIT"

"I'VE BEEN THROUGH ALL THE FLOORS
— IN ABOUT THREE SECONDS."

" IT HAS ITS POINTS . IT WILL KEEP YOUR MOTHER-IN-LAW AWAY. "

" INDOOR PLANTS, MY FOOT! THAT'S DRY ROT. "

" ON THE OTHER HAND I DON'T
SEE ANY RISING DAMP "

" I'D RATHER YOU DIDN'T LOOK,
MRS. PRENDERGAST. JUST
CALL THE POLICE. "

" YOU'LL NEVER GET A MORTGAGE! "

" I WAS WRONG! IT'S IN EXCELLENT CONDITION."

RIPE FOR CONVERSION

" BELIEVE IT OR NOT, THIS PLACE USED TO BE A PIG-STY. "

" JUST IGNORE IT. IT'S ANOTHER LOCAL SMART-ALEC. "

" WHOSE IDEA WAS IT, TO CONVERT AN OAST-HOUSE ? "

" I'VE UNEARTHED ANOTHER RAILWAY SANDWICH. "

" IF HE ASKS US TO TAKE A PEW AGAIN, I'LL SCREAM. "

" I DON'T LIKE THE WAY YOUR BROTHER TIPS ME, ON THE WAY OUT. "

" RESTORING AN OLD PUB WAS A MISTAKE. "

" DON'T TELL ME!   IT USED TO BE A STABLE.   RIGHT? "

" YOU'LL HAVE TO GET RID OF THE SAILS. THAT'S THE THIRD TIME MY
NIGHTIE'S BEEN CAUGHT IN THE MILL STONES. "

" IT WAS ORIGINALLY BUILT AS A LABOURER'S COTTAGE. "

" YOU'LL BE SLEEPING IN THE FAGGOT OVEN "

" DO YOU MIND NOT USING THE SINK WHILE I'M PAINTING THE BOTTOM ? "

" THERE'S A FOOT OF WATER IN THE LOUNGE
BUT STILL NO ELECTRICITY. "

A COTTAGE FOR THE WEEK-END

"THAT DAMNED LOCK'S RUSTED UP AGAIN."

" IT WAS PROBABLY JUST THE BLOOD CURDLING SCREAM OF A VIXEN."

" DON'T PANIC. IT'S ONLY A COW. "

" YOU BROUGHT THEM. YOU TAKE THEM BACK "

" IT WOULD HAVE TO BE THE BOSS'S WIFE. "

" MAY WE BORROW YOUR MOWER ? "

" I GOT ABOUT HALF AN HOUR'S SLEEP BETWEEN
THE NIGHTINGALES AND THE DAWN CHORUS. "

"THE MILK'S ON THE STEP"

" GOOD HEAVENS, EILEEN! HE WONT HURT YOU. "

" THAT WRETCHED CUCKOO'S BEEN HERE AGAIN. "

" HE'S PINCHED YOUR FISH FINGERS "

" I'LL GET A CUP OF TEA WHILE YOU TIDY UP THE GARDEN."

" LOOK HERE, MR. QUAGMIRE! THESE FREE RANGE POULTRY OF YOURS....."

" IN THE BATH! LOOK AT THE ONE IN THE BATH."

" IT WAS **MY** TURN FOR TEA IN BED THIS MORNING. "

HOUSE WARMING

"ONE OF THEM HAS TO GO! THE CONVECTOR HEATER OR THE BUDGIE."

" I TOLD YOU TO DUST IT BEFORE YOU FIXED THE DOUBLE GLAZING. "

" I CAN'T SEE ANY HEAT ESCAPING THROUGH THAT LOT. "

" HAS THE THUMPING NOISE STOPPED ? "

" LEAVE IT OFF ! YOUR FATHER'S HAD THE ELECTRICITY BILL."

" IF YOU DON'T LIKE THE SKIRTING HEATERS, WHY DON'T YOU JUST SAY SO."

" YOU'LL BE SETTING THE THING ON FIRE WITH YOUR CIGARETTE ENDS. "

" YOU TAKE CARE OF YOUR CONTRAST AND VERTICAL HOLD.
I'LL LOOK AFTER ROOM TEMPERATURE CONTROL. "

" MAY WE BORROW A DROP
OF FUEL OIL ? "

" FIVE YEARS OLD LAST TUESDAY
AND CAN'T TELL THE TEMPERATURE ? "

" I THINK IT'S THE THERMOSTAT AGAIN. "

" ME TARZAN — YOU JANE . "

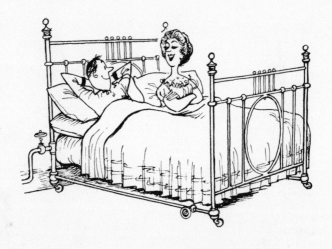

" I'VE GOT TO ADMIT IT, YOU'RE BRILLIANT. "

HOME
IS WHERE YOUR HEART IS

" THEY'LL NEVER GET ME UP IN ONE OF THOSE THINGS. "

" ...OF...NO...FIXED...ABODE... "

" THERE'LL BE A HERD OF CATTLE SOMEWHERE WITH OUR GROCERIES. "

" HELLO! THE DEATH DUTIES HAVE BEEN PAID OFF. "

" TAKE IT EASY CHARLIE. THAT WHEEL SQUEAKS. "

" HENRY! PLEASE! THEY'RE
OUR BREAD AND BUTTER."

"WE'VE OFFERED HIM ALTERNATIVE ACCOMMODATION."

" I PREFER TO LIVE IN SOMETHING WITH A BIT OF CHARACTER . "

"WHAT CHANCE OF HAPPINESS HAVE CHILDREN GOT IN A PLACE LIKE THIS.?"

"I'VE ALWAYS ENVIED THEIR IRRESISTIBLE URGE TO BE ON THE MOVE."

" WAKE UP, FRED. WE'VE GOT BURGLARS. "